To my Mother and Father.

Author's Foreword.

As promised in my previous book, "St. Agnes Parish 1850-1920", I have now produced a companion volume covering the period 1920-1950.

Once again I have relied heavily on postcards from professional photographers; improved techniques in this era made cameras both easy to carry and operate and at the same time brought them within the reach of the pocket of the layman. A debt is owed to those who took the trouble to record events in our Parish 40 and 50 years ago, which were every day happenings then, but are now of historical interest and are only recorded in books such as this.

Many readers of my first book have told me how much pleasure and enjoyment they obtained from it. I hope this volume gives all just as much enjoyment. Some readers will find pictures showing themselves as children, or young people, and they will, I hope, bring back happy memories of yesteryear.

UNDER ROYAL PATRONAGE

B. Eves

"ST. AGNES"

Down, down in old St. Agnes,
   Down by the silvery sea,
Where waves are ever rolling,
   Tossing the foam so free.

Here shady lanes are clustered
   With ferns and grasses green,
And merry birds all twittering
   Upon the bushes seen.

Points, the weathered old Church spire,
   Close by the winding street,
Where cottages and gardens fare,
   With wayside meadows sweet.

Down the long and rocky path,
   Where pretty sea-pinks grow,
Watching the old wheel turning,
   Fixed on the stream below.

Paddling round the sea-weed rocks
   The children often rove,
Tucked up, with spade and bucket,
   Digging in sandy cove.

Away upon the beacon,
   O'er heather, gorse, and stiles,
Viewing the sea and country,
   Mines, stacks, and shafts, for miles.

And when the moon is shining,
   On thatched old roofs and trees,
You hear the old owls cooing,
   Perched up among the leaves.

Down, down in old St. Agnes,
   Beside the rumbling sea,
Wrapped in with Mithian's beauty,
   A pretty spot to see.

Shops and Street Scenes

Vicarage Road, St. Agnes about 1920, and looking very different from today. The road is unmade, and note the cobbled pavement in front of the shops.

The first shop on the left was a tailor's owned by Richard Rilstone, but known locally as "Tailor Dick". The second was Arthur Reynold's Grocer's Shop, who was advertising a wide variety of goods including Westward Ho Smoking Mixture, Reckitt's Starch and two brands of tea, Lyons' and Lipton's.

Beyond the General Supply Stores and next to the Railway Inn, the shop was, for many years, a Dairy and Greengrocer's owned by Mr. John Kidd Smith later to become a greengrocer's and fruiterer's owned by his son, Mr. Tredinnick Smith.

A very rare view taken in the late 1920's of the cottages and shop on the site of the present day "Diversions" Bookshop and Minty's Cottage. The cottage furthest away in the row is a shop, which, at the beginning of the century, was a Tobacconist and Sweetshop run by Mrs. Sarah Blackney. From 1923 to 1927 it was Mr. Dunstan's first Chemist's shop in St. Agnes. Most of us will remember it lately owned by Mrs. Borlase, selling her lovely ice-cream served with a big wooden spoon. She retired in 1977, aged 93, and the shop was converted into a dwelling. To the left of this shop can be seen the building of the shop adjoining Dale's Garage. Mr. Dale built his new garage and also demolished the cottage that had been next to it and built the present shop. The old cottage is visible in the photograph on the front cover.

This picture shows the shop built on the site of the two cottages mentioned above. In the early 1930's the shop traded under the name "Brown & Medlock" and local people still refer to it by this name. This picture was taken in the late 1930's and shows Mr. Brown outside his shop. Note the advertisement board for the Daily Herald, a newspaper no longer available, along with the Daily Sketch and News Chronicle. You could also find postcards for sale; he was the local agent for Judges postcards. The man posed in the street is Mr. Matthew (Mathee) Hodge, the village undertaker and carpenter.

Vicarage Road on a sunny day. Stanley Johnstone Williams has a good display of ladies hats in the window of his milliner's and draper's shop. No difficulty for the driver of the car, registration number RL 7797, to park outside. The picture was probably taken about 1929. The premises, then occupied by Mr. Williams, now form part of the chemist's shop.

Mr. Arthur Reynolds outside his Grocer's and Provision Dealer's shop in October 1926, on the opposite side of Vicarage Road from his former premises. The window display to the right of the entrance is advertising "Free, footballs for boys and dolls for girls" in connection with Nelson's Gelatine Lozenges. In the other window is an advertisement for Lyon's Sausage Rolls, cakes and pastries. Apparently not everyone made their own.

St. Agnes Wesleyan Sunday School and Band of Hope Tea Treat procession at the top of Rosemundy Hill in 1920. Everyone wears either a hat or cap, and a couple carry raincoats; well it might rain, even on Tea Treat day. The building on the right is a Bakery and Tobacconist's, with the entrance in Rosemundy Hill. In 1927 it became a Chemist's and remains so.

Frederick John Gribben in the entrance of his shop about 1930. A versatile chap combining the trades of Ironmonger, Cycle Agent, and Hairdresser. An advert of his in a guide book of the time reveals that he had a private room for Ladies Hairdressing, and amongst his goods for sale were a variety of ladies' and gentlemen's toilet requisites, a large stock of paints was kept and he could also provide prams and push chairs.

This excellent photograph was taken by Mr. S.J. Govier of Chacewater. Mr. Bragg of Falmouth, whose fine work is a feature of my first book, died shortly after the end of the first world war, and we are fortunate that Mr. Govier continued to record village life in such a professional way.

Apart from the disappearance of the buildings at the top of British Road, and the state of the road, the view has changed little today. Note how everyone is motionless, posed for the photographer, even the horse.

A feature of the village was the cobbler's shop kept by Mr. Butcher opposite the Miners' and Mechanics' Institute, illustrated here with a picture taken after 1950, but still showing the building as it was when the older men used the shop as a popular meeting place to discuss the events of the day. Today Miller's Estate Agents occupy the site.

The unknown photographer who recorded St. Agnes Band leading a procession along Vicarage Road would not have foreseen the changes that were to take place in this part of the village. He has captured a rare view of Numbers 15 and 16 Vicarage Road, the cottages that were demolished in the late 1950's when Trelawny Road was built to provide access to the new council estate.

Another unusual view this time taken from inside the Mushroom Tea House. Although the picture was taken after 1950, it records a scene that had been unchanged for years and is now gone. The cottage on the left of the lane, which led to fields, was owned by Mark Hellyer, who had succeeded Matthew Hodge as the village undertaker.

The Regal Cinema, whose attractions included "The Desert Rats" and the "Silent Voice". Behind the newer entrance to the cinema is the Oddfellows Hall, built in 1881, at a cost of £600 for the St. Agnes Lodge. It was used for various public entertainments before its conversion to the Regal in 1933. The cinema closed in 1978, and became the Little Puppet Theatre, until converted to its present day use as a restaurant.

Note the advert on the wall of the house on the right, for "Sanpic. There's a fragrant hygenic". Used in the cinema perhaps?

No. 23 Vicarage Road in 1930, when it was a newsagents and sweetshop run by Violet Whitta, who remained there until 1934 when she moved to her new shop in Churchtown. She also sold gramophone records, the window display on the right of the doorway being devoted to those of the Columbia label.

These two photographs show Moris Davis in Vicarage Road in 1928. Moris worked at the bakery in Churchtown and as a young man it was his job each morning to go to the fields behind Lloyds Bank to collect the horse and donkey to pull the carts which delivered the bread. Moris would walk through the village leading one animal with each hand, and when they came to Whitta's shop both animals would refuse to move until Mrs. Whitta had given them each a sweet.

The Terrace about 1920 showing John Angwin's stationers. At the rear of the house were his print works, which were taken over in the early 1930's by Josiah Sidney Repper who remained there until 1939 when he moved to new premises at Churchtown. Note the engine house of West Kitty Mine on the right and the dormer window in the roof of Enysvilla on the left.

The square at Churchtown around 1928, when the present day "Pins & Needles" shop was a gentlemen's outfitters owned by Edward Mark Uglow. The house adjoining provided board and lodgings, a young waitress has posed for the photographer in the doorway. The lady standing and the gentleman sitting on the seat marked "Private" could be the owners. On the windowsill of the upstairs room nearest Uglow's are a pair of shoes probably freshly whitened and left to harden in the sun.

Churchtown Stores in 1937 when owned by the Radcliffe family as a Draper's and Grocer's shop. Note the postcards in the window of the door of the left hand shop, also the advert for "Flexcello Hosiery", anyone remember this? The advert on the far right of the picture, on the wall above the bicycle, suggests we should eat Batchelors Peas. Rex Radcliffe is the boy standing outside the shop which has changed little today, excepting the brand names of goods sold.

Mr. Hawke of Helston took this photograph and produced a postcard which was bought in August 1924. He had a motor car and travelled extensively in both Cornwall and North Devon taking pictures for his postcards.

No. 6 Churchtown in the right foreground, was the home of the Gripe family. Until 1910 it had been a shop, and the old frontage remains. In 1932 Alfred G. James opened a boot and shoe shop there, and today it is Lee & Co., Estate Agents.

Mr. Govier produced this postcard of Churchtown about 1920, when the White Hart was a Free House kept by George Reynolds. Paull's Hotel placed an advert in the 1925 guide for St. Agnes when they boasted of "excellent cuisine, modern sanitation," and possessed a garage.

The shop on the right of the picture was a butcher's, as it is today. The adjoining property was residential until the 1930's when it was converted into a tobacconist and confectioner's.

Note, the Lychgate at the entrance to the Church has yet to be built, which was done in 1935 in memory of George Coulter Hancock, a former County Councillor for St. Agnes, and amongst the other Public Offices he performed was that of Clerk to the St. Agnes School and Burial Boards.

This postcard shows the alterations mentioned above. The butchers shop hasn't an extensive display of meat, only a few sausages and a single joint in the window. His advert beneath the window exhorts his customers to "Eat Colman's Mustard with our prime beef, mutton, etc. and enjoy the more".

Mrs. Whitta stands in her shop doorway between the two newspaper advertisement boards, for the Morning Post, and News Chronicle, neither obtainable today. The Daily Telegraph announces that its paper contains "Duce's Terms for a Truce", no doubt referring to Mussolini's invasion of Abyssina. The Daily Herald contains "Templegates" Newmarket Selection, which probably sold more papers in the village!

A 1925 postcard looking towards the Bakery. The shop in the centre of the photograph was owned by Mr. W.H. Cowl who had the bakery next door, where according to his adverts, he made "High Class Cakes" and "Allinson and Bermaline Bread". When this picture was taken the shop was a draper's, but about 1926 Mr. Cowl took possession to use as a restaurant and tea room. It was later used as a Gift Shop, but was completely destroyed by fire on 12th November 1972, the land on which it stood being unused until 1980 when the present shop was built on a similar design to the one destroyed.

Mr. Govier took this photograph in the 1920's capturing the apparent tranquility of everyday life. He has managed to persuade everyone on the hill to pose for him including the council workman with his wheelbarrow, who took a rest from clearing the ditches.

A quiet time in Peterville around 1928 showing the wide open area used for many years as the centre of activities. The remains of the dissenters' meeting house, built in 1780, can be seen where the Peterville Garage is today.

A lorry loaded with Pratt's Paraffin is parked at Peterville, was the driver delivering to the villagers, or had he gone for refreshment in the Peterville Inn?

QUAY VALLEY AND BEACH

Quay Valley about 1923, and looking very short of vegetation compared with today. This postcard was sent to Sidmouth on the 2nd August 1923, with the sender writing "I am charmed with the place and such comfortable lodgings; we have struck oil in every way, thanks to you. I am writing this from on top of the Beacon."

The flats at Trevaunance Cove shortly after conversion by Mr. E. Tredinnick, about 1922. He advertised in the West Briton for Masons, Carpenters, and Labourers to convert the former Marine & Mining Store, and because of the high unemployment 70 people came from as far away as Rose, Goonhavern, and Perranporth for an interview at Mingoose. To try and alleviate distress he only employed those men who were not eligible for dole money.

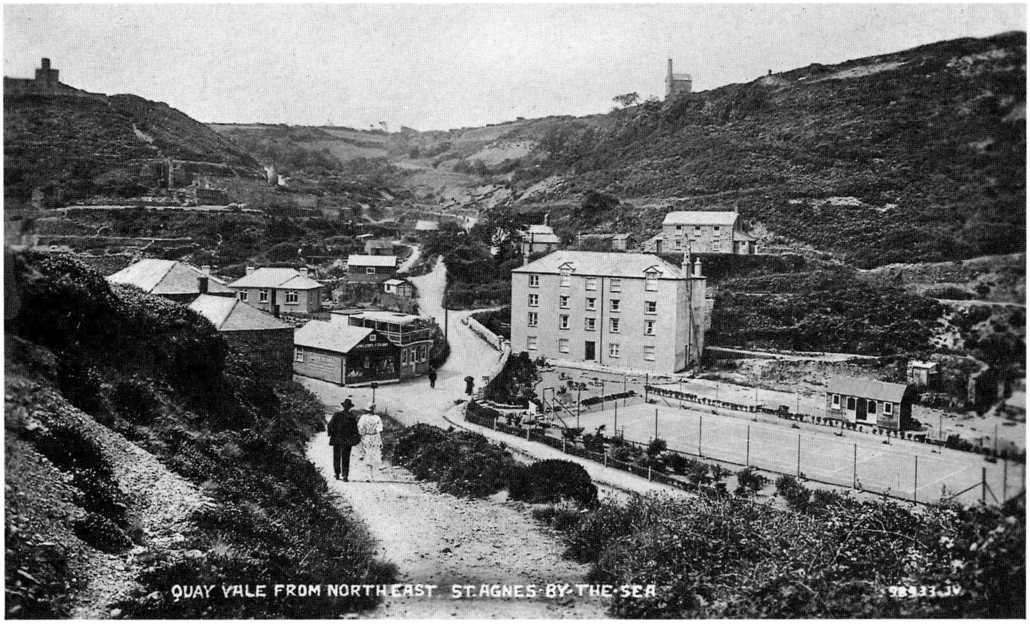

This postcard was posted on 19th July 1928, and the writer is complaining about the awful heat. The picture shows Quay Valley towards Rocky Lane, and Kemp's Store and Tea Rooms are in the centre, at the bottom of Rocky Lane.

In the 1925 guide to St. Agnes they advertise "Teas and Ices served on the roof garden overlooking the Tennis Court and bay. A new hard Tennis Court where you can enjoy this popular game close to the sea and beach, 2 shillings per hour including use of balls."

Anyone for tennis? Mixed doubles with all players in their best whites at Kemp's Tennis Court, an earlier view than the picture shown above, taken before the small pavilion was built.

No yellow lines to prevent the occupants of the fine open top car from viewing the game from the roadside. Note, all the boys watching from the grassy bank are wearing caps. The band is preparing to play in the background, unlike Wimbledon, where the band stops before the tennis begins.

Fishermen preparing their boat on St. Agnes Beach in the mid 1930's. The second Beach Cafe with its distinctive roof which was used as a tea garden, is at the top of the beach.

When this photograph was taken around 1920,the Harbour had all but fallen down, with only part of the wall nearest the camera remaining. The once thriving little cove seems very quiet compared with twenty years ago. Mining was dying and the buddles visible in front of the foundry, in the foreground, would soon be removed, the only industry remaining being that of tourism.

Chapel Porth

This picture of Chapel Porth taken by an unknown photographer, was sold as a postcard by Treseder & Son, Brooklyn Cafe & Stores, Porthtowan, and posted on a "really wet" 30th August 1925. It shows Chapel Porth as it looked for many years after the cessation of mining, and before the increase in motor vehicles made it necessary to build a car park. Two vehicles have managed to get into the picture, parked by the roadside.

Visitors were getting to Chapel Porth in the mid 1920's in sufficient numbers to encourage Mrs. Lillie Davis who had a shop at Goonvrea, St. Agnes, to open a summer tea room. Mr. Govier visited there in 1927 and produced a postcard showing her standing in the doorway. Mrs. Davis probably commissioned him and sold the cards in her little business. Patrons could either lounge in a deck chair, or sit at the table on some very smart looking chairs.

Mr. Hawke visited Chapel Porth on a busy day in the mid 1930's, the car owning tourists had arrived. The mine workings have been levelled to make a car park and several people can be seen swimming and surfing in the sea.

In the foreground are the remains of the old water wheel used to power mine machinery around the turn of the century. Mr. John Henry Murrish's Ice Cream Hut has been erected at the car park entrance.

A postwar view of Chapel Porth, the car park is now almost full, it is interesting to note the number of people on the road walking to the Porth.

Mr. Murrish's Ice Cream Hut has been replaced by Claire Donald's larger Tea Hut, Claire also hired out surf boards.

Dawn on 18th November 1928 revealed that the 687 ton Liverpool registered coaster, the "S.S. Eltham", en route from Swansea to Rouen with Welsh Coal, had by some mischance been wrecked on Chapel Porth Beach. All the crew of 14 were missing, and none were ever found. A lifeboat was washed up on the beach at Chapel Porth, and another at Perranporth. Wrecks of this type were quite common in the days of sailing ships and unsophisticated methods of navigation, but were not expected in the late 1920s. Mr S.H. Richards, a newsagent with a shop in Vicarage Road, St. Agnes, recorded this scene; each onlooker no doubt had their own theory as to how it had happened, a couple even brought their dogs.

The young Bill Morrison stands on the wreck during the summer of 1929, with him is Willie Webb from Praze.

The only remains of the wreck visible today is the black boiler which can be seen on the Porthtowan side of the beach at low tide.

Mingoose

A sunny early spring day probably about 1930, found Mr. Hawke journeying to Mingoose, and photographing this peaceful rural scene. A good day for drying the washing in the back garden. Over a 100 years ago the scene would probably have been more lively as the building on the left nearest the camera was a Public House called the Miners Arms. It remains a residence today.

A horse drawn wagon ambles its way up the hill out of Mingoose towards Towan Cross in this postcard, which was sent on 27th May 1932 from St. Agnes to a Mrs. J. Berryman in a place called Corning in Canada. Did this picture make her long for home?

BLACKWATER

Blackwater village, a view taken around 1920. Note the semaphore signal on the railway protecting the approach to Chacewater Station, such signals are disappearing rapidly from the railway scene today. Between the railway and the village mining spoil is evidence of the industrial past, no sign of any bypass.

T. Dennis Jenkins' shop in the early 1930's. The adverts include their own brand of tea, and the White Star Dominion Shipping Line to Canada.

There is no evidence of the shop today, the shop front windows have been replaced to match those of the upper floor, and Wheal Concord Mine took over the premises to use as their offices.

West End in the 1920's. The road winds under the railway bridge of the Chacewater to Newquay Branch Line. The late Mr. John Oates left a legacy of beauty to Blackwater village in the rhododendrons he planted on the high embankment near the bridge. In early summer they provided a colourful sight for travellers on the main road as well as on the trains.

The cross roads, another view taken in the 1920's. A boy leans against the sign post pointing to Chacewater chatting to his friend. Another direction post indicates the way to the station, which although called Chacewater was as near to Blackwater as to its named village. The motor age is catered for by the garage with its petrol pumps and the promise of repairs, but the young boy riding his bicycle towards Chiverton appears to be ready to mount the pavement to avoid the oncoming car; cyclists would need to take more care on the road before long.

The two photographs on this page show the improvement of the main road in the 1920's. Mr. Govier took this picture not long after the end of the first world war. Horse drawn transport outnumbered motor powered vehicles and the muddy unmade road was sufficient.

Only a few years later and Mr. Govier was back again to record the changes. The road has been widened, and given a tar macadam finish. Pedestrians have been given a pavement, and Mr. Wilfred T. Nott has opened a garage. Other than painting a centre white line, this road had to cater for ever increasing volumes of traffic until the new bypass was opened in the summer of 1988.

Mount Hawke

A man spends a few hours fishing near the old Mill at Mount Hawke, while the two ladies look on, perhaps hoping for one for tea. The Old Mill in the centre of the picture was driven by a water wheel and had its own water course from the Gover Valley. Today the mill has been converted into a dwelling.

Mr. R.A. James owned the grocer's shop on the left of the picture, but the ownership of the van, registration number YY9465 hasn't been ascertained.

Although the growth of motor traffic had necessitated the "School" warning sign, the only vehicle in sight is a horse and cart behind the postman.

The building projecting towards the road in the left background is the Blacksmith's Shop, run by Montague Rodda. The small garage on the right, behind the two ladies catching up on the gossip, belongs to the Methodist Minister.

A view taken looking the opposite way from the one above, the girl on the cycle is having a struggle to get up the hill.

The small Post Office serving Mount Hawke village. Mrs. Mary Chynoweth was the sub postmistress in the 1920's. Only limited facilities were available, if you needed to buy a money order then it was a trip to either Blackwater or St. Agnes.

Miss Muriel Rowe's Mount Hawke Stores, now converted to a dwelling, where 4 ounces of winter mixture could be bought for one penny. (Winter mixture were boiled sweets.)

Porthtowan

Looking down the valley into Porthtowan between the wars, still relatively undeveloped compared with today, but vast changes have taken place since the photograph shown on page 30 of my first book. Development is starting to take place on the high ground above the Porth.

A Cornwall Motor Transport bus at Echo Corner, Porthtowan, probably in 1926. This bus route operated from Perranporth to Redruth via St. Agnes, Mount Hawke, Porthtowan and Wheal Rose four times a day. The fare to Redruth from Perranporth was 2s6d return ($12\frac{1}{2}$p) and from St. Agnes 2s0d (10p). Cornwall Motor Transport were taken over by the National Omnibus Company in November 1927.

Behind the bus is a cafe advertising Lyons' Tea, with a couple of caravans and a tent outside. Porthtowan was always popular with campers.

Two lovely old buses seen in the village, though when the picture was taken they were the new means of transport that was opening up such villages both for the visitor and the resident, privately owned motor transport still being a rarity. The single decker was on the Perranporth to Redruth service, and the double decker is likely to have come from Camborne.

Until 1926 the buses only went as far as Echo Corner, but following complaints the route was extended into the village.

Visitors to Porthtowan around 1920. There seems to be three generations, with grandma relaxing in one of the deck chairs, father supervising from the doorway of the well built hut, and the children lying on the grass. It looks like a motor cycle and sidecar well protected with a tarpaulin behind the tent, never trust the weather.

These two pictures depict a crowded beach on a Bank Holiday in the late 1920's when crowds descended on Porthtowan particularly from Redruth and Camborne. This day out was the highlight of the summer, many people brought a picnic with pasties, saffron buns and heavy cake. For those who were still hungry there were ice cream stalls on the beach, most drawn by a donkey, enterprising traders set up stalls selling such delicacies as Tom Trot. Note, in the bottom picture, a large crowd on the left, possibly watching a Punch and Judy Show.

Another view taken on the same day as the previous two pictures. This visit to the beach was a time for adults to bring themselves up to date with family news and gossip whilst they were watching the children playing on the sand and paddling in the many rock pools. Some of them as we can see, even went as far as rolling up their trousers, or removing their stockings and "Washing their feet". Not the lady with her back to the camera, centre right, who would appear to have brought her fur, and looks to be dressed for a shopping trip to "Town".

A bathing pool was first proposed in 1912, an experiment being made at the Tobin Rock side of the beach, but this was found unsuitable because of the shifting sand.

In 1915 a meeting was held in Miss Gill's Tea Room and Mr. Beringer, a Redruth jeweller, produced plans proposing the rolling of large rocks forward for the cove to form a retaining wall. The rocks were to be keyed and bonded with lime and sand mortar. It was to be high enough to retain sufficient water to be able to dive or swim. The position also ensured it would be flushed at every tide. The plans were adopted, and the pool remains today.

Mithian

Mithian around 1925, photographed by Mr. Hawke who has driven from Helston in his Morgan car and parked it near the Mens' Institute. This building was begun in 1893, by the villagers, but they could not afford to complete the work. Mr. Passmore Edwards made a donation and this enabled the building to be finished.

Further down the village on a different visit by Mr. Hawke. There is nothing on the back of the card to tell us why the "X" is over the Old Manor House, which is the oldest building in Mithian, being built before 1550. It is now divided into five cottages.

The building to the right of the picture is Mrs. Edith Mabel Ennor's grocer's shop, an advert by the entrance is for Lipton's Tea. This shop is now a dwelling.

One of six photographs taken for a firm called Regal Art Publishing Company, of London, who then sold them to local traders. Mr. George Symmons who owned the shop pictured, agreed to order some of each. Someone made a mistake in processing the order, and instead of receiving a few of each view, several boxes of each of the six were delivered. They had to be stored all over the house using every spare bit of space that could be found, and some were even used by Mr. Symmons as notelets. However, when the American Servicemen came to Trevellas during the war, the cards were suddenly in great demand to show the folks back home how lucky they were to be in such a beautiful place. With inflation Mr. Symmons could increase the price, and instead of sustaining a heavy loss, he finally made a pretty profit on the deal. The car in the foreground CV9421, was registered in 1932, so the picture dates from shortly after this. There is an advert for "Board Residence" on the wall of the house where the other car is parked.

A view, taken a few years earlier than the one above, when Mrs. Rogers kept the village shop, and looking towards the Miners Arms Public House. The pub is reported to have been built in 1577. This 16th century inn has many interesting features including decorative plaster ceilings and a Penance Cupboard. There is also a secret passage that leads from the Inn towards the Manor House. It is stone lined, but a villager who went down the tunnel many years ago said the centre portion had collapsed under the road.

I have not been able to accurately date this postcard, taken by a Redruth photographer Mr. W. Caddy, and it is possibly pre 1920. It shows a young girl standing by the gates of Rose-in-Vale House, which is now a Hotel, but when a private residence was the home of both a Doctor and a Mine Captain. A gentleman is wheeling his bicycle up the hill possibly on his way to catch a train at Mithian Halt on the Chacewater to Newquay Branch line, which served St. Agnes and Perranporth.

4th June 1927, Mithian Women's Institute, which was only a few months old, holds its first fete, on a beautiful Whit Saturday. Mrs. Lavin and Mrs. Crebo are behind the stall. Freda Crebo and Keitha Rice stand in front next to Miss Ichet who is holding two baskets of fruit. Tom Dyer puts a restraining arm on the shoulder of a young Roy Lavin. The rest of this group are, from left to right:- Roy Harris, Jack Chapman, Marshall Brokenshire, Annie Tredinnick, Alfred Solway, Norman Sexton, Dick Harris, Roy Tregellas, and Cecil Tregellas.

The building of Mithian Church Tower in May 1928.

This was the second tower the Church had built. The original tower was built with the Church in 1898, the steeple became unsafe and was taken down with the tower. The stone used for this tower came from Wheal Daniel, a gift from Lord Falmouth.

The Vicar at the time, Rev. P. Phelps, is standing proudly in the doorway, obviously pleased with the way the work was progressing, whilst the workmen have stopped to pose for the photographer, Mr. Govier.

The remains of Jericho mine as seen through the lens of a visitor's camera on the 28th August 1925. Situated about a mile from St. Agnes it was used as the stamps and tin dressing plant for West Kitty Mine. Ore worked from under the village was transported here by horse and cart.

Trevellas Porth in the 1920's.

Tin streaming works are clearly visible in the porth where men were still making a living from the waste washed down from the mines further up the valley.

Many people when they think of Trevellas Beach, think of Blue Hills and their Easter Saturday visit to watch the London to Lands End motor trials. This particular section was introduced in 1926 by Donald Healey of Perranporth, and is still used although, in recent years, the trial has ended here instead of Lands End.

This view, taken prior to 1937, shows the old route the cars took up to the left, on the present day main road. This was later considered to be "too easy", and the new route was introduced up the cliff path seen in the top right of this picture.

Contestant No. 148 just manages to negotiate the bend on 30th March, 1932. Policeman Greet is on hand however to assist should the need arise, as are the St. John's Ambulance men.

It takes the combined efforts of the rider, a Constable of the Cornwall County Constabulary, and an official of the Motor Cycling Club to get this machine moving up the hill; the next rider is already approaching in the background.

Cross Coombe Farm became a casualty of world war in 1941 after it was compulsory purchased by the Air Ministry for the building of Trevellas Airfield. The photograph shows the rear of the Farm House which backed onto the old road that went to Trevellas Porth.

A young girl on the pony called Tommy drives the cows along the road towards Trevellas Porth, assisted by the farm dog. Behind her is the old Cross Coombe Sunday School and Chapel, which remained for a while after the airfield had been built, but when it became necessary to extend the runway, they too were demolished.

Farming

In the yard of Cross Coombe Farm about 1928. The farm had three working horses, Victor, Albert & Jessie, and it was the responsibility of Harold Dark, pictured astride one of his charges, to look after them. The farmer, Mr. Northey stands with the pony, Tommy, pulling the trap behind him.

Three horses pull the reaper and binder at Beacon Farm St. Agnes in 1935. As the machine moved forward the corn was cut, and the sail brought the cut corn onto a canvas conveyor which carried it to the rear of the machine where it was tied and knotted by the knotting machine. It was then deposited on the ground ready for stooking.

By 1937 the horses at Beacon Farm had been replaced by a Standard Fordson Tractor. Modernisation may have replaced the horses, but the same number of men are needed to harvest the crop. The tractor had steel wheels and a wooden hinged band was placed around them for travelling on a road.

Mr. Northey the farmer at Cross Coombe Farm, in the 1920's, driving a horse drawn hay rake.

The driver sat in a shapely cast iron seat from where he could operate hand or foot levers to raise or lower the curved tines. The hay was pulled into piles before being loaded onto the hay wagon.

This lovely harvesting scene was taken at Beacon Farm in the 1930's, and shows straw being loaded onto the horse drawn wagon. Two ropes are seen hanging from the rear which were used to secure the load as it was carried down over the hilly fields to the yard where the rick was made. The coastline beyond Perranporth can be seen in the distance.

A well loaded wagon of hay at Cross Coombe Farm in 1926. Piles of hay have been made in various parts of the field using the hay rake. The two men on the ground are using pikes to throw it onto the wagon which the horse will then pull to the rick.

A straw rick is being built here at Cross Coombe Farm in 1926. After the corn has been through the threshing machine and the grain removed the straw is ready to be made into a rick to be used later.

Several chickens can be seen under the wagon, no doubt hoping to find the odd grain of corn dropping off the straw.

Here a Hay Grab is being used to pick up the loose hay from the wagon and load it onto the rick. The grab was attached to a jib which was operated with twin pulleys on a long pole, the loose end of the rope being attached to a harnessed horse. As the horse was led away from the pole, the grab lifted and closed. When it had reached the required height it was swung over the stack by one of the loading team and tripped to release the hay. The horse was then reversed back to the rick to repeat the process, a manoeuvre which most horses greatly disliked.

Cameron Estate was built at the beginning of the second World War on the cliff edge between St. Agnes Head and Chapel Porth. Originally it was used as a Coastal Defence Battery with gun enplacements on the side of the Beacon. However in 1944 it was occupied by the 10th Anti-aircraft Battery under the command of a Lt. Colonel. Its role was to train crews in the use of the Bofors Anti-aircraft guns, and the trainees included American servicemen, with up to 2,000 being there at a time. Joe Louis the World Champion heavyweight boxer is reported to have spent time here. After the war the camp was used as housing accommodation until sufficient houses were built by Truro Rural District Council in St. Agnes village. Today the camp has completely disappeared, the land has returned to downs and is used as a picnic area.

Eight Servicemen relax outside their billet on St. Agnes Beacon.

The third from the left is George Langford, the others aren't known. Can anyone help? The bases of the huts are still clearly visible, and if you stand there today you can appreciate what a panoramic view these men would have.

These people were not going to let the war spoil their day out at Chapel Porth. Barbed wire fortifications are at the top of the beach, and large concrete boulders seen behind the group are the remains of the wall that stretched across the width of the beach as a deterrent to a possible enemy landing. A narrow gap was left, however, to give access to the beach.

The people are, from the left: Tom Battershill, Mrs. Battershill, Ethel Whitford, Valerie Morrison, Joan Morrison, Kathleen Morrison, Christine Berryman (Morrison) and Ken Lambert.

Trevellas Airfield

The building of this airfield in 1940 caused the demolition of many farms, cottages and mine buildings, but it was needed as a base for fighter aircraft to assist in the protection of the convoys of ships coming into the Western Approaches. When 66 Squadron arrived in March 1941 to be the first to use the airfield, work on its construction was still taking place, and only one runway was available, which caused many problems if the wind was blowing from an unsuitable direction. Before accommodation for the servicemen was built on and near the airfield, they lodged at the Droskyn Castle Hotel at Perranporth, with a large marquee at the airfield for the use of those on standby.

Bawden Rocks off the coast were used by pilots for target practice. After the war the airfield closed, and the arable land was used by local farmers; the runways remained, and in the late 1950s the Cornish Gliding and Flying Club was formed. Their use of the runways continues to the present day.

It does not appear from the second world war air raid records that any deliberate air attacks took place on Trevellas aerodrome, unlike its neighbours Nancekuke and Penhale Camp. Odd bombs fell in Perrancombe and at Goonhaven, but these no doubt were strays jettisoned by bombers making a run for home. By the end of 1941 all enemy air attacks had ceased in the St. Agnes area.

Two different ways in which an attacking aircraft MIGHT be shot down at Trevellas; above a Bofors Anti-aircraft gun manned by three, very relaxed looking personnel, and right; a lone serviceman with a Lewis gun on the perimeter of the airfield. He is in a vulnerable position.

St. Agnes Air Raid Wardens, winners of the Divisional A.R.P. Cup.

The men are:- (left to right) John King, A.J. Roberts, John Arnold, Sam Hocking, Tommy Waters, William Morgan Andaine, Alf James, Jim Britt Rickard, Jack Symmons and ?

"Dad's Army". Trevellas Home Guard.

Back Row: (from the left) Ambrose (Joe) Beckett; Fred Brokenshire, Jimmy Green, Jim Vincent, Sidney Dark, Clem Wills.

Middle Row: Cyril Mannell, Harold Dark, Clifford Mitchell, Jack Holmes, Arthur Cornter, Philip Hooper, Henry Ford.

Front Row: Howard Hooper, Leslie Shugg, Hedley Roberts, Frank Moore, George Symmons.

November 1942, dancing at the Masonic Hall. An opportunity for the many servicemen stationed in the Parish to let their hair down on a Saturday night and meet a few local girls.

The war over, this was one of the last military parades held in the parish. The occasion was on the 3rd July 1949 when Field Marshall Wavell and other dignitaries took the salute at the British Legion County Rally in St. Agnes.

Transport

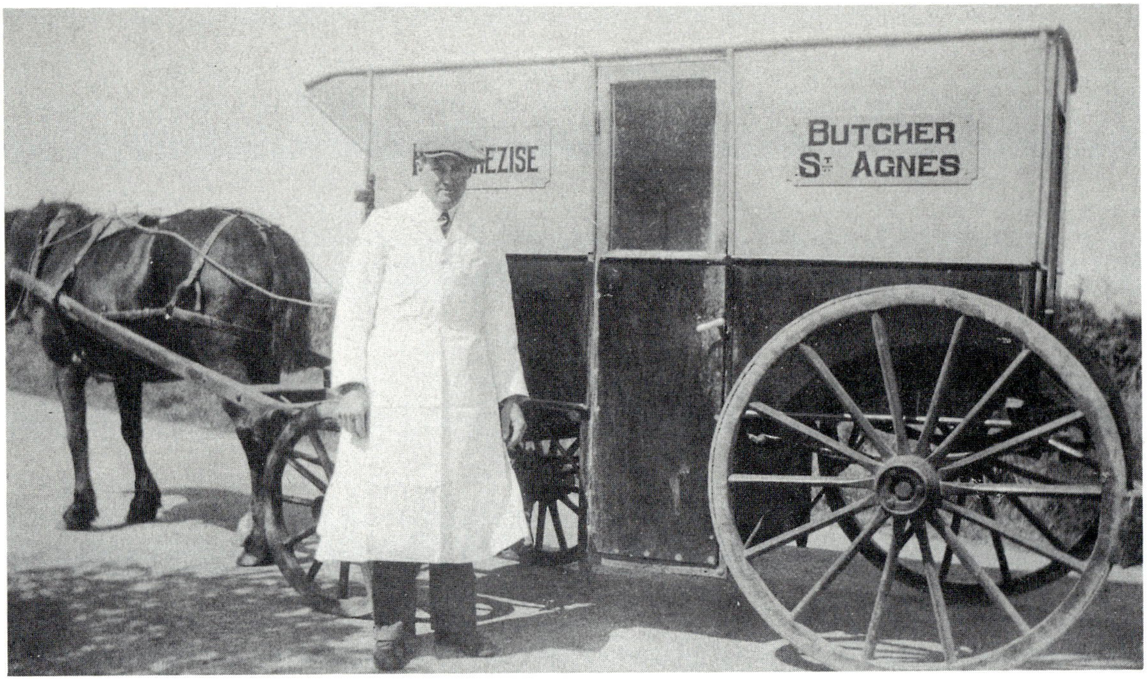

Edward Austin Trezise with his butcher's wagon in St. Agnes, the picture thought to have been taken in 1940. He ran his business from his farm at Goonbell, where he had a slaughter house and cold room. On a Saturday people went to his farm to buy meat, but the rest of the week he went around the village selling from his wagon.

A pony and jingle at St. Agnes railway station in the 1920's. Before the motor bus services were developed and the arrival of the motor age, a jingle or trap was a widely used means of transport. With the station being so far from the village most long distance passengers finished their journey in one or the other.

The donkey in this picture is the same animal as that shown with Moris Davis earlier, and has been snapped at Peterville pulling Mr. Cowl's baker's barrow in 1925. Originally this was a hand barrow, but modernisation took place; shafts were attached, and donkey power replaced man power much to the relief of the man who previously had to push it around the village.

Vincent's ice cream cart on Mingoose Hill in 1933. The two boys buying ice cream are Bobby and Russell Fowler. The wafer biscuits were supplied by Huntley & Palmers.

Dale's Garage in the early 1930's. Mr. Dale and a customer stand by a Vauxhall car Registration XX3617, used by Mr. Dale as a taxi. A chauffeur poses next to his employer's Daimler. Note the large starting handle, and AA Badge, which would be saluted by their Motor Cycle patrolmen.

Kellow's bus outside St. Agnes Church en route to Truro about 1927. This was the first St. Agnes owned bus to travel to Truro and its owner, Ivan Kellow, stands beside it, and would no doubt drive it. Note the canvas roof pulled back today, but cover was available should it be wet. This was competition for the train, but the big advantage was, it started in the centre of the village, no long walk to the station.

AF632 is a grey 12HP Lizare Et Naudin, and was owned by Mr. Willie Newton, who kept the public house and garage at Peterville. Mr. Wright of the Castle Hotel, Launceston, was the original owner in January 1911. This photograph was taken in the 1920's; the man on the motor cycle on the left of the picture is Mr. Jim Britt Rickard.

Bill Morrison took this photograph in 1948 and shows Sam Hocking of Higher Goonvrea Farm at Chapel Porth driving his converted 12HP Austin. Nicknamed "Jitter Bug", the car was normally used for cartage purposes around the farm with just the occasional longer outing to Chapel Porth.

An accident at Town Hill, St. Agnes in the late 1940's. The three wheeled Singer owned by Mark Yelland from Mingoose collided with the stone support when it met the other car coming down the hill in the narrow section.

Note where the 30 m.p.h. speed limit ended at this time.

Sunday, 11th May 1947, in the field owned by Doctor W.C. Whitworth behind Vicarage Road, was the scene of a special service conducted by the Vicar Rev. G.H. Barnicoat, and handing over ceremony of their new ambulance to the St. John's Brigade. The vehicle was named "St. Agnes" by Miss Tremearne, whose family had contributed over half of the £925 needed to purchase this 26 Horse Power Vauxhall. Mr. John King stands posed for the photographer having officially accepted the ambulance on behalf of the local Division. Unfortunately the vehicle acquired a reputation for being difficult to drive due to a very light suspension, which also made it less comfortable for the patients than expected from a new model.

A group photograph taken after the dedication service for the new St. Agnes St. John's Ambulance on 11th May 1947. Pictured are, from the left:-

John King, Dr. Cuthbert Whitworth, Richard Grigg, Fred Olds, Douglas Mitchell, Mr. Hooper, Fred Nicholls.

John Hooper, Roy Francis, Claude Lockett, Bert Skewes, Clifford Grigg, Stanley Williams, Dr. Henry Whitworth, Bill Woolcock.

St. Agnes Band lead the Flora Dance at Peterville in 1948. After the war the Band were without uniforms, but were to look as smart as they had before the war when new uniforms arrived in 1949.

Friendly Retreat had been converted from the mine dump and rubbish heap for Wheal Friendly Mine, and Saturday 12th May 1923 saw most of the shops closed in the afternoon so that their employees could attend the opening of the new park. St. Agnes Band, seen on the right of this photograph, had, under their bandmaster Mr. A. Soloman, led a procession from the school, the children and their teachers forming the bulk of the participants.

The gates were officially opened by Mr. W. Harris of St. Agnes, who was a pioneer of the scheme. In the grounds an outline of the scheme was given by Mr. J. Angwin, and he is thought to be the gentleman on the platform in the picture. He was deputising for Mr. R.P. Ratcliffe, Chairman of the Parish Council and the Town Improvement Committee. Mr. R. Whitworth and Mr. W.J. Kemp both living in Truro, but each had lived in St. Agnes, gave a seat, and if the weather hadn't been stormy the proceedings were to have concluded with a Promenade Concert; this was substituted with a concert at the school. One event which did go ahead was a football match, St. Agnes v Old Crocks.

This entertainment in the Men's Institute at Blackwater had two performances on Wednesday 27th and Saturday 30th December 1922, and the programme included Christmas Carols accompanied by the Blackwater Orchestra.

St. Agnes Wesleyan Sunday School Tea Treat procession in Vicarage Road, on July 17th, 1920, an occasion for wearing and showing off your best clothes, lucky it's a beautiful day.

The Tea Treat procession has now reached Peterville, time to stop and give the band a rest. The boy on the right of the front row leans wearily on his Union Jack. How much further do we have to walk?

GROUPS

ST. AGNES PRIMARY SCHOOL FOOTBALL TEAM 1949-50.

Back Row: (left to right) Graham Blackburn, Cyril Woon, David Drew, Alec Hoskins, Ronald Hicks and Kenneth White.

Front Row: Mr. Soloman, Arthur Ellis, Rupert Carter, Malcolm Rogers, Patrick Nankivell, David Boundy and Mr. Hearn.

ST. AGNES BAND 1949, displaying prizes won at the Stenalees Band Contest.

Back Row: Alf Kneebone, Clifford Bolitho, Frank Roberts, Tony Williams, Tony Oliver, Ken White and Ron Matthews.

Middle Row: Austin Tremain, Cecil Tremain, Ray Gribben, Reg Leach, R. Williams, Maude Juleff, Bernard Gribben, Dot Juleff, Desmond Russell, Carlos Robins.

Front Row: Russell Berryman, Clifford Williams, Gerald Willcocks, Frank Moore (Bandmaster), Edward Eley, Frank Kneebone, Charlie Chegwyn.

BLACKWATER COUNTY PRIMARY SCHOOL FOOTBALL TEAM 1948-49.

Back Row: (left to right) Mr. Best (Teacher), Bazil Roberts, Richard Collins, Willie Nicholls, Donald Menhennet, Fred Coombs, Gerald Lobb, Mr. Garland (Teacher).

Front Row: Ivan James, Trevor Whitford, John White, Leslie Wills, Trevor Glanville and B. Moore.

Played 12 games, won 11, lost 1. Goals for 63, against 9.
Goal Scorers:- White 36, James 11, Roberts 6, M. Davey 8, Lobb 2.

THE COMMITTEE OF BLACKWATER MENS' INSTITUTE BOXING DAY 1923.

Back Row: Jacker James, Jack Sando, Arthur Moyle, Wilfred Nott, Tommy Oates, Jack Coad, and P.C. Stephens.

Front Row: Ernie Smith, Frank Harris, Charlie Davey, Willie Davey, Leslie Maddern, and Raymond Tippett.

Mithian Womens Institute 1927 and 1948

Mithian Womens Institute Fete on Whit Saturday — 4th June, 1927, attracted a large attendance, helped by good weather.

How many, I wonder, were also in attendance at the 21st anniversary celebrations held in the W.I. Hall at Barkla's Shop in 1948. There are too many in this photograph to name individually, but many faces will be familiar to local residents.

MITHIAN COUNTY PRIMARY SCHOOL, CLASS I, 1926.

Back Row: (left to right) Douglas Mitchell, Croydon Nankivell, Willie Gilbert, Bazil Stephens, Eldred Brokenshire, Clifford Harris, Sydney Stephens, Henry Harris, Douglas Chapman, & Miss Roskrow.

Middle Row: Phyllis Roberts, Hazel Retallick, Enid Harris, Edna Bending, Freda Crebo, Winnie George, Peggy Parsons, Ruth Morcombe, Ester Herrin, Joan Miller.

Front Row: Willie Jennings, Stanley Harris, Henry Gilbert, Herbert George, Terrence Barnicoat, Roy Bending, Clyde Bartle, Maurice Chapman, Jack Mitchell.

ST. AGNES COUNTY PRIMARY SCHOOL, CLASS IV, 1947.

Back Row: (left to right) Andrew Thomas, Frank Johns, Derek Parnell, Ernest Robinson, Roy Marsh, Gerald Symmons, Terry Nankivell, Ian Beard, Donald Sibthorpe, Richie Allen.

Middle Row: Robert Johnson, Tony Heath, John Harper, Maureen Cowling, Jennifer Matthews, Betty Bunt, Mary Richards, David James, Christopher Williams, Alan Thomas.

Front Row: Veronica Potter, Elizabeth Bunt, Gillian Webb, Mildred Williams, Anne Mitchell, Margaret Chatterton, Angela Thomas, Cynthia Cowling, Margaret Butson, Sally Stevens.

Acknowledgements

In compiling this book I have had assistance from numerous people.

I would like to thank the following for the use of their photographs:-
Mr. William Andain, Mrs. Freda Male, Mr. Moris Davis, Mr. Robin Kellow, Mrs. Langford, Mrs. Jeannette Martyn, Mr. Douglas Mitchell, Mr. George Mitchell, Mr. Johnny Murrish, Mr. Roger Radcliffe, Mrs. Beryl Thomas, Mr. Bernard True, Mr. Malcolm Rogers, Mr. Bill Morrison, Mr. John Redfern.

Thanks also to Mr. Frank Carpenter for the information from his book "The Story of a Village Street", to Mrs. Win Carpenter for proof reading the text, and especially to Mr. Roger Lacey for his support and hard work in helping to compile and research the book, as well as the hours spent in typing the text.

Finally, thanks are due to the many people who helped with information for the text, too numerous to mention individually.

Rear Cover Photograph:
Mithian W.I. Fete, 5th June 1927.
Mrs. Walker, Dorothy Walker, Freda Crebo, Roy Lavin, Dulcie Chapman.